RAISING VEGETARIAN CHILDREN

How To Raise Happy, Healthy, Vegetarian Kids

KATE ANDERSON

© 2015

D1309954

"A man can live and be healthy without killing animals for food; therefore, if he eats meat, he participates in taking animal life merely for the sake of his appetite."

Leo Tolstoy

Contents

How To Raise Happy, Healthy Vegetarian Kids

Raising happy, healthy vegetarian children is easier than you might think and might have been lead to believe! Vegetarian foods are delicious! And what's more, children raised on plant-based diets have been proven to be healthier than meat-eating children. Yes, proven. But just like any other diet, there are certain things you need to know when it comes to keeping your little one healthy. Whether your child is a newborn or a teenager, taking the steps to find out how to keep them healthy is something every parent should do and this book will tell you everything you need to know.

Most parents of vegetarian children would agree that the hardest part about raising vegetarian kids is actually other people's opinions. Often times, our friends and family pay extra close attention to how quickly our vegetarian child grows or scrutinise us every time they catch a cold. And sometimes it seems like people just can't wait until your child expresses the simple truth that "bacon smells good".

"But she WANTS it! I can't believe you would DEPRIVE your child of food! Think of how left out she feels in front of all the other kids!"

Before I get into a rant about how many times I've heard sentences like this and how completely nonsensical they are, I'd like to start this book by saying: **you have every right to make decisions about your child's diet regardless of the opinions of others**. As long as you take the time to ensure your child is getting the nourishment they require (which is *much* easier than people think), you've got to let other people's opinions fall off you like water off a duck's back. Raising a vegetarian child sometimes requires you to develop a thick skin in the face of adversity! But it is worth it, stick at it if it is what you believe in.

This text covers everything you need to know about feeding your vegetarian child from babyhood to university. Whether your child has been a vegetarian from the very beginning or recently became one, this book will teach you the vital nutrients your child needs in their every day meals and snacks as well as how you and your child can deal with other people's opinions! In addition, I will give you some unbeatable tips about picky eaters, packed lunches, parties and celebrations, and much more. You will also find a meal plan for children of all ages and a number of nutritious and delicious recipes your kids will absolutely love!

Part One: Putting Your Child's Health First

Parents of vegetarian children often get a lot of slack and mocking from other people. Sometimes it seems like everyone has an opinion about your choices and they insist on expressing them whether you've asked or not. Whether it's judgment from a concerned grandparent or disbelief from your friends, every vegetarian parent needs to grow a thick skin fast when facing the masses. Later in this book I will discuss many practical ways you can ease other people's concerns and turn any unwanted or negative attention away from your child's eating habits, but for now I'm going to focus on the most important thing: your child's nutritional needs. This is number one.

There are some truly fantastic health benefits of living as a vegetarian. Far too many people believe that vegetarian children will grow up to be underweight, sickly, vitamin deficient, or deprived of things they "need". Absolute nonsense! Contrary to popular opinion, a child living on a well rounded vegetarian diet could easily be far healthier than their meat-eating counterparts. It's a well known fact that vegetarians have lower risks of diabetes, heart disease, high blood pressure, and even certain cancers. Furthermore, studies have shown that vegetarians have a significantly reduced chance of suffering from childhood (and adult) obesity. Children who are fed a varied plant-based diet naturally take in more water, fibre, plant proteins, and complex carbohydrates, while taking in less saturated fats and cholesterol. Generally speaking, vegetarian children have been shown to be of a leaner build and have a lower BMI than meat-eating children. Studies have also shown that children who are fed plant-based diets have a better understanding of food and are therefore, more likely to have healthy diets in adulthood, which as a parent will likely be something you are concerned with. The decisions you make for your children now could drastically change their entire future.

The P word! For some reason, most parents of vegetarian children (along with their family and friends) focus a lot of attention on *protein* in the child's diet. If you grew up with an overbearing parent constantly stressing the importance of protein in your diet, chances are, now that you're all grown up they'll start focussing that stress on your child. Parents of vegetarians often get quizzed about how they are going to make sure their child gets enough protein. It seems like there's a rumour going around insisting that meat is the only source of protein! Well, I'm happy to tell you that is simply not the case!

Protein is certainly necessary for muscle growth and making hormones and enzymes, but it is much easier for vegetarians to get than most people think. You can rest assured that protein exists in a variety of plant-based foods. The most important thing is to remember is to feed your child a varied diet. Every diet - vegetarian or otherwise - is healthier when it has plenty of variety. If your child is in a particularly picky phase, fear not! There will be plenty of focus on picky eaters later in this book. For now though, try to include a few different sources of protein in your child's diet each week for optimum health. The following list contains some of the richest sources of protein in the vegetarian kingdom.

Protein In The Diet: 15 Ideas

1.) Milk, eggs, and other dairy products
It's not just meat that contains animal protein! Other animal sources like dairy and eggs have protein as well! If your child is a lacto-ovo vegetarian, chances are their daily life is already full of protein and you have nothing to worry about. One common misconception is that vegetarians have to eat a lot of cheese to get enough protein. Beware this misconception! Cheese has a significantly high fat content and should be eaten - like most things - in moderation.

2.) Nuts

Nuts are a vital part of a vegetarian diet. They offer large amounts of protein among a number of other vitamins and minerals. Nuts can be added to cereals, baked goods, salads, or spread on toast or sandwiches in nut butter form. Research regarding the safety of nuts and nut butters in infants and toddlers has been divided for a long time and it is entirely up to you whether or not you feed them to your young child. However, if you do decide to feed your baby nuts, remember that whole nuts are a choking hazard and should not be given to children until roughly five years of age. Stick to nut butters or recipes with ground nuts to ensure safety.

3.) Quinoa

This protein-rich grain is a fantastic base for salads but it can also be used in stews, breakfast cereals, granola bars, and more. Quinoa is naturally gluten free too, so it can be a great alternative to things like pasta and couscous for gluten intolerant people. Quinoa is also available in flour form so can also be used in baked goods!

4.) Soy

Vegetarians have been turning to soy for its naturally occurring protein for decades. Soy proteins can be found in tofu, dairy replacements such as soy milks and soy yoghurts, edamame beans, and tempeh. It is important to note however, that soy should not be used as a primary source of protein in your child's diet. Too much soy can cause adverse affects on your child's body including hormone disruption and growth problems. To be as safe as possible, choose fermented soy products such as tempeh, miso, and tamari (fermented, gluten-free soy sauce) and keep the intake of any unfermented soy products to a minimum to be on the safe side. Steer clear or using soya formula for your infant unless absolutely necessary.

5.) Chia

These tiny seeds are packed with goodness. In addition to the significant amount of good quality protein they contain, they're also full of omega-3 fatty acids, fibre, and a number of other very important nutrients. You can use chia seeds sprinkled over cereals or salads, or you can include them in your baked goods, puddings, smoothies, and protein bars. The best thing is, if you've got a picky eater, this seeds are so small, they're likely to go undetected in your child's favourite breakfast cereals or snacks!

6.) Beans and Lentils

This doesn't just include kidney beans and lima beans! There are tons of different types of beans that are packed with protein, many of which are easy to implement into even the pickiest child's meals. Beans can be used to make burgers, Mexican rice and beans, bean dips, veggie chilli, burritos, and a number of other yummy meals. Lentils are also very easy to "sneak" undetected into your child's soups, sauces, and even pizza!

7.) Chick Peas (Garbanzo Beans)

Packed with protein and very versatile, chick peas are most vegetarian parent's best friend. You can use chick peas in hummus, stews, or on salad. You can use them for sprouts, bake them into a crunchy alternative to store bought salty snacks, or buy them in flour form to make breads and other baked good!

8.) Seeds

There are a number of seeds which contain protein and a lot of other nutritional goodness. Sunflower, sesame, poppy, and pumpkin seeds are all great sources of protein. Pumpkin seeds in particular make a great snack as they taste delicious and are one of the healthiest foods on the planet. You can get seeds into your child's diet by sprinkling them over cereal or salads, mixing them into baked goods and protein bars, or simply toasting them and coating them in herbs and spices. You can even grind seeds into a thick powder to use in baked goods.

9.) Dark greens

Getting greens into your child's diet is important for a variety of reasons but most people don't realise how much protein they actually contain. Dark, leafy greens like spinach, kale, and chard are excellent sources of protein and so are other green vegetables such as broccoli, asparagus, and peas!

10.) Cauliflower

This is one of the most surprising protein-rich vegetables. Most of us were told at some point in our lives that light coloured vegetables offered very little nutritional benefit. It turns out, that's just not true. Cauliflower is a great source of protein, omega-3s, and many other vitamins. And cauliflower needn't just be boiled and lobbed onto your kid's plate! You can use cauliflower as a base for cheesy pizza, soups, salads, and more.

11.) Non-Dairy Milks
If your child doesn't drink cow's milk, there are naturally occurring proteins found in most non-dairy milks (not just soy milk!). Almond milk and rice milk contain protein and can be used over cereal or blended into smoothies and milkshakes for an extra protein boost!

12.) Seitan
This meat substitute is a great source of protein. It can be used in sandwiches, stir fries, and tons of other meals. Seitan is made from wheat gluten so it is nut suitable for people suffering from gluten intolerances.

13.) Cocoa Powder
Yes that's right! Unsweetened cocoa powder contains a decent amount of protein and quite a few other vitamins and minerals. Popping a spoonful or so into a smoothie might mean your child gets a little hidden nutrition in their favourite treat!

14.) Oats
Oats are great for lots of reasons. In addition to the surprising 6.08 grams of protein per cooked cup, they also help stabilise blood sugar levels, and offer a number of other vital minerals. And don't worry if your child doesn't like oatmeal! You can use oats in protein bars, granola, and many other baked goods.

15.) Microprotein
This is a mushroom-based protein found in certain brands of meat substitutes. If you cook with meat substitutes containing microprotein your child is guaranteed a good hit of protein. Meat substitutes are especially good for children who have become vegetarian later in life as they might miss the taste of meat.

However, if your child has been vegetarian from birth, they might be reluctant to eat processed food flavoured like meat. It's entirely up to you and your child. As you've seen there are plenty of other great sources of protein to be found in plant-based diets.

The next time anyone talks to you about protein in a vegetarian diet you can easily refer to the above! Now that you're well equipped to fight the protein battle, it's important to focus on all the other vitamins and minerals that play an integral part in your child's health. When it comes to health, it's rarely protein that vegetarians are lacking. Rather, the most common deficiency found in vegetarians is **iron**. Before I go on, I must urge that, if you are ever concerned about your child's health or growth in any way, **seek medical advice**. Your family doctor should be informed of your child's vegetarian diet. This will ensure that they will test for vitamin deficiencies if necessary and they will be able to offer you sound medical advice if and when you need it.

Because the iron found in plant sources is considerably more difficult for the body to absorb than that which is found in animal products, it's vital that you place enough importance on the iron available in your child's diet. You can make the iron found in plant sources much easier to absorb by simply coupling it with another food or drink that contains vitamin C. Serve your child's iron-rich meals with a glass of orange juice, tomato sauce, or a handful of strawberries for dessert and you can be sure your little one is getting all the iron they need. The following list covers some iron-rich foods to keep in mind when planning your child's meals.

10 Vegetarian Sources of Iron

1.) Whole grains
Wholewheat breads, pasta and brown rice are naturally rich in iron as well as plenty of other vital nutrients. Simply switching to wholegrain varieties of your child's favourite grains will help fight

anaemia as well as offering extra fibre and regulating blood sugar levels.

2.) Dark leafy greens
Spinach, kale, collard greens, broccoli, brussels sprouts, and most other dark green vegetables are packed with iron. It may seem impossible to get these veggies in your child's diet if they're a picky eater, but you can easily "sneak" these iron sources into your child's meals by blending them into soups, smoothies, and sauces. One thing to remember is that, though plant sources of iron are best when coupled with vitamin C, both spinach and broccoli are good sources of iron *and* vitamin C which makes them perfect choices for iron!

3.) Raisins and other dried fruits
These chewy snacks are one of the tastiest sources of iron for vegetarian children. Raisins, dried apricots, prunes, and dried peaches are all fantastic sources of iron and fibre. Sprinkle them on your child's breakfast cereal or yogurt and couple them with a handful of strawberries or orange juice and your child has the perfect breakfast! Dried fruit is also an easy snack to carry with you when you're out of the house so they're a fantastic alternative to sugary store-bought snacks!

4.) Oats
If your child likes oatmeal, they are probably already getting a decent amount of iron in their diet. Oats are a great health food. They offer protein and iron and help maintain blood sugar and keep the mind alert. You can sprinkle some raisins onto your child's morning oatmeal for an even more iron-rich breakfast. If your child doesn't like oatmeal, try them with granola, or bake your own granola bars, oatmeal-raisin cookies, or other yummy treats!

5.) Lentils
These legumes are a fantastic source of iron and protein. There are a large variety to choose from and make a great addition to salads, soups, and sauces. If your child doesn't like the look of lentils, simply blend them into their favourite soups and sauces and they won't notice a thing!

6.) Beans

Pinto beans, black beans, black-eyed beans, soy beans, and others all contain iron, protein, and fibre. They're a staple part of a vegetarian diet that not aren't only packed with healthy nutrients, but they also keep tummies full for longer. Baked beans, bean burgers and dips, chilli, and bean salads are all easy to make, delicious, and healthy.

7.) Tahini

This sesame paste is most commonly used in hummus but can also be used in sandwiches, on toast or rice cakes, sauces, and salad dressings. Tahini is absolutely packed with iron! Making your own hummus at home is a great way to implement it into your child's diet. You'll find a simple recipe at the end of this book.

8.) Potatoes

Potatoes are a surprising source of iron *and* vitamin C. They can serve as a carefree source of iron as they are so versatile and most children love them. Cook them any way you like, but do beware of allowing your child to eat too much deep fried foods like french fries as too much added fat could affect your child's health.

9.) Tofu

Tofu is another very versatile vegetarian food. Many people don't like tofu because of its bland flavour, however, tofu is a great alternative to scrambled eggs, can be used in desserts like cheesecake, or marinated and skewered at a BBQ.

10.) Pumpkin and Sunflower Seeds

Both of these seeds are fantastic sources of iron as well as a number of other vitamins and minerals. Toasted or raw seeds make a delicious snack. Mix them with some nuts and dried fruit as the perfect snack when you're on-the-go, or sprinkle seeds over cereal, granola, oatmeal, or salads for a crunchy addition to one of your child's favourite meals. You can also mix seeds into baked goods like muffins, banana bread, and granola bars.

Nutritional Needs

Lacto-ovo vegetarians are at relatively low risk of malnutrition; however, it is important for parents of vegetarian children to make informed decisions about what they feed them. Because children raised on plant-based diets aren't exposed to the more readily available vitamins and minerals found in red meat, poultry, and fish, it's important to pay close attention to what they are consuming on a daily basis. Be conscious of things like sweets and fizzy drinks in your child's diet and be sure to keep them to a minimum. This is not just because they are unhealthy and may form bad eating habits; it's also because candy, cookies, cakes, and sugary drinks could fill your child's belly quickly, meaning they won't be hungry enough to eat the vitamin-rich meals you place in front of them. This is especially true for babies, toddlers, and smaller children. Later, I will give you some helpful hints on how to keep treats to a minimum and offer you some more specific advice about the nutritional necessities of children at different ages. But before I move on to the next section, take a look at this last list of *vital* nutrients your child needs.

5 Vital Nutrients Your Child Needs

1.) B12
This B vitamin is very important for your child's growth, brain development, the functioning of their brain and nervous system, and the formation of red blood cells. Lacto-ovo vegetarians should consume enough B12 each day if they are eating a sufficient amount of eggs and dairy products; however, if your child is adverse or intolerant to dairy, it's important to pay close attention to their exposure to this vitamin. Though there has been a discovery of B12 in certain seaweeds and algae, unfortunately, it's not possible for humans to digest. If your child is vegan or intolerant to dairy, feed them fortified foods such as cereals, breads, non-dairy milks, and meat substitutes. Another food packed with B12 is Marmite brand yeast extract. This can be added spread on toast or added to soups or sauces. Parents of babies and toddlers who are breastfeeding needn't

worry about B12 as there is plenty available in breast milk. Deficiency of B12 can cause depression, fatigue, memory loss, and other long term and irreversible effects to your child's body functions so if you have any concerns about your child's intake of B12, seek medical advice immediately.

2.) Calcium and Vitamin D
Calcium plays an important role in the strengthening of your child's bones as they grow. It also aids the function to muscles and nerves as well as helping the release of hormones and enzymes in your child's body. Children that take in plenty of dairy products generally get all the calcium they need; however, if your child gets into the habit of drinking sugary drinks or juices, they may become reluctant to drink milk. If milk isn't on your child's list of favourites, you can be sure they're getting all they need by offering them plenty of fortified juices and cereals, green vegetables, tahini, almond butter, sweet potatoes, beans, and lentils. It is important to remember that in order to absorb calcium properly, you child needs exposure to vitamin D. There are very few food sources of vitamin D available to vegetarians however, you can find it in cow's milk and fortified foods like those listed above. The easiest way to get vitamin D into your child is by making sure they get enough sunlight. Just spending 15 to 20 minutes outside each day should be long enough to get them all they need. If you are concerned about your child's exposure to the sun, speak to you doctor to discuss supplements.

3.) Omega-3's
This fatty acid plays an integral part of your child's cognitive development and growth. Studies have shown that babies and children who are fed enough omega-3's have longer attention spans, better hand-eye coordination, better social skills and a decreased risk of asthma, diabetes, and depression. If a child continues their exposure to omega-3's into their adulthood, they may have better heart health and have a decreased risk of developing certain cancers. Though most people insist that the best source of omega-3's is fish, there are plenty of plant-based sources available. Feed your child plenty of seeds (namely chia and hemp seeds), dark leafy greens, squashes, and beans (mung beans are best), your child should be getting all they need!

4.) Zinc

Zinc is an essential mineral which plays a major role in your child's growth, the health of their immune system, creating DNA, and repairing body tissues. A child eating plenty of seeds, nuts, whole grains, beans, lentils, and dairy products should be getting all they need on a daily basis. However, beware a diets with a high fibre content as too much fibre could prevent your child from absorbing zinc as well as calcium and iron. To make zinc easier for your child's body to absorb, soak dry beans, brown rice, quinoa, seeds, and nuts for a few hours or overnight. This process not only makes zinc easier to digest, it also increases the total nutritional value of your food!

5.) Fat

Fat is an important source of energy in children; especially younger children. It is important not to confuse fat with sugar and deep fried / greasy snacks. The types of fat your child should be exposed to is that which is found in full fat milk and dairy products, nut butters, seeds, avocados, sweet potatoes, and soya-based meat substitutes.

As I have mentioned before, vegetarian children tend to grow up to have healthier eating habits than their meat-eating counterparts, but this is greatly reliant on you as a parent. As your child grows, include them in meal planning, teach them the importance of healthy eating, and encourage them to be creative with food. Though most children do go through a picky phase at some point or another, it's important to continue to offer them a variety of new foods and flavours to encourage them to grow out of their pickiness and become a bit more daring with their meals.

Part Two: The Growing Vegetarian

As children grow up their nutritional needs change and so do their experiences. Whether you have an overly judgmental family or your child is faced with difficult situations in school, raising a vegetarian can be tough at times. This section focuses on your child's changing needs. It covers topics such as picky eaters, packed lunches, birthday parties and other celebrations, and how to approach difficult social situations. It also includes meal plans for every age.

This section is broken up into two parts - infants and toddlers, and then school age children and teenagers - so that you can easily refer to the parts that are relevant to you as your child progresses through life and the different eating stages they face.

Vegetarian Infants and Toddlers

Children who are raised on a vegetarian diet get a wonderful start to life! They are generally healthier than meat-eating children and are far more likely to develop lifelong healthy eating habits. Raising your child as a vegetarian even extends their life expectancy, fact!

As an infant, the best thing for your child is breast milk. Breast milk contains absolutely every nutritional need your baby has. In addition to being natural and convenient, breast milk also boosts your baby's immune system, soothes and comforts them, and creates a healthy sense of security and emotional stability. However, breastfeeding is not possible for every family and if your baby is formula fed, they should be receiving everything their body needs for the first few months of their life.

The First Foods

Most parents wean their babies onto solid foods at some point around the age of 6 months. Because your baby will still be receiving breastmilk or bottle feeds, this early stage of solid foods is less about nutrition and more about teaching your baby how to chew and swallow and exposing them to new flavours. Some parents find this stage quite troublesome but it really shouldn't be with the correct advice. However, there are some foods that are more beneficial than others in these early days.

Your baby's first foods should be finely pureed and vitally important that it should not contain any lumps to avoid choking. I recommend that you introduce one food per week rather than feeding them many different foods too soon which can be a bit of a shock to a babys delicate palette. The other advantage of introducing one food at a time is that if your baby has an allergy, stomach upset, or any other adverse reaction, you will know which food caused it.

So what should come first? I recommend you start by introducing rice cereal. You can mix this up with breastmilk or purified water but remember not to make it too hot! If your baby is breastfeeding, they will be used to food that is body temperature and no warmer. Something that is too hot could startle your baby and leave them reluctant to eat solids again.

When you're ready to introduce a new flavour, you can choose from most fruit and vegetables but you may wish to avoid certain things. For instance, if your baby is breastfeeding, they will have a natural "sweet tooth" because breastmilk is quite sweet. You might benefit from starting your breastfed baby on vegetables that aren't sweet like potatoes, parsnip, and swede. You can mix a little breastmilk (or formula) into any food to make new flavours taste a little more familiar. Other vegetables that are great starter foods are carrots, peas, squash, pumpkin, and sweet potatoes. Once you have introduced vegetables you can start to combine them to make new flavours. There are plenty of fruits that young babies love too. Apple, pear, and banana are all a good place to start.

Top Tip: If your baby suffers from reflux, avoid acidic foods like oranges, apples, and grapes as these could cause tummy upsets!

When it comes to baby food, I am a big believer in making your own. Though jarred baby foods may be more convenient, they contain preservatives and are highly processed. Feeding your baby homemade fresh foods will provide them with a higher nutritional value, shield them from any unwanted additives, and help them develop a taste for healthier foods right from the start. And you'll save time and money!

To make your own baby food, simply follow these 6 easy instructions:

Homemade Baby Food 101

1.) Wash, peel, and deseed your fruit / vegetables and make sure all cooking and storing equipment is clean and sterilised.

2.) Boil, steam, or bake a large batch of fruit / vegetables.

3.) Puree in a food processor adding some of the nutrient-rich cooking water until you have the desired texture (thin and smooth for young babies, lumpy for older babies).

4.) Spoon into ice cube trays and freeze.

5.) Once frozen, put the frozen cubes into airtight bags / containers, label with the date, and keep in freezer until you need it.

6.) Thaw and heat in a microwave or stove-top or hot water.

Top Tip: Only make a large batch of baby food when you know your baby likes it, to avoid waste! (all new babies LOVE waste...)

Making and storing your baby food this way is a great way to save time and money and keep your baby in great health. You can even take these little frozen cubes of baby food with you if you're going out for the day so there's no need for store-bought convenience foods! Other foods that travel well (and do not require cooking) are soft fruits that you can mash with a fork like banana, avocado, mango, and melon. Remember to never add salt, sugar, or sweeteners to anything you feed your baby!

Foods for Toddlers

Feeding your toddler can be a lot of fun. At this stage your baby is old enough to have a better understanding of food. They will delight in "helping" you in the kitchen and trying new things. One of the best ways you can get your child interested in healthy foods is by allowing them to take part in the food preparations. Don't worry, I'm not suggesting that you encourage your toddler to use knives or play with fire! But I am suggesting that you talk with your child about the foods your offering them. Talk about where they come from and how they grow. Think about growing some edible plants in your garden or on your kitchen windowsill and give them the job of watering the plants. Have your child get ingredients out of the fridge when you're preparing a meal or have them help you tidy up afterwards. Activities like this encourage your child to engage in the world around them and respect where food comes from. They also increase your child's attention span, expand their knowledge, and help them develop better social skills. Young children are capable of more than most people give them credit for. They respond well to intellectual stimulation and being involved in daily business.

When planning a meal, let your toddler pick between two choices. This will engage them in the meal planning and give them a sense of control. Resist the urge to ask questions like, *"What do you want for lunch today?"* as this is too broad with possibilities and you might end up with an unexpected and undesirable answer! Instead, offer your toddler a choice of two things that you deem feasible. Say, *"Do you want beans and toast or hummus and cucumbers for lunch?"* Children delight in making choices and giving them specific options makes it easier for both of you. Remember that in order to create long-lasting healthy eating habits, it's best to start right from the beginning.

So too, it is important that you make mealtimes happy, fun, and interesting. Often, parents put too much pressure on their child at mealtimes. They get upset when the child doesn't eat enough or doesn't behave the way they want. This type of contention around the dinner table could cause further mealtime disturbance as your child ages. Try not to nag your child throughout mealtimes and try not to become upset with them if they don't eat everything on their plate. **<u>Never</u> use food as a reward or punishment. This is one the biggest mistakes parents make when trying to raise healthy happy vegetarian children.** Bribing children with dessert or sweets is a bad habit and it almost always backfires as the child ages. Having bad experiences with family mealtimes at a young age could cause an unhealthy relationship with food in later years.

Instead, make mealtimes a time when you engage with one another. Talk to your child at the dinner table and let them talk to you. Remember that children eat slower than adults and they will have days where they eat less than others. Meal times should be a peaceful and social time; not one with shouting, screaming, or threats. If your toddler seems to eat less than they should, think about what they have eaten in a whole day rather than what they've eaten at one meal. For instance, they may not have eaten the carrots on their dinner plate, but they may have had carrots with hummus as a snack earlier in the day. They may not like the quiche you serve at dinner but they might've already had an egg at breakfast and some greens for lunch. The bottom line is, **don't panic and cause a huge scene!** Small children will not starve themselves. They will eventually eat! Furthermore, children who were breastfed are more likely to stop eating when they're full than bottle-fed babies. This is because breastfed babies feed on demand and stop eating when they're full whereas bottle-fed babies are often encouraged to eat more than they're hungry for because their food is measured. Children who eat little and often will digest their food better and have less stomach upsets than those who are encouraged to eat three large meals anyway so try not to stress yourself and your child out by making dinner a source of contention.

Note: Both breastfed babies and vegetarian children have been found to grow at a slower rate than bottle-fed babies and meat-eating children; however, if you have any concerns about your child's health or growth rate, seek medical advice.

In order to be sure your toddler gets plenty of nutrients throughout the day, make sure all their snacks are packed with nutritional value. Healthy snacks are particularly important for vegetarian children as it may take more quantity of vegetarian food to equal the nutritional value of meat (for instance, chicken vs beans). Resist the urge to give your small child sugary or salty snacks. There is absolutely no reason for a baby or toddler to eat sweets and you can be sure that the more unhealthy snacks you give them, the more they'll want and the harder it will be to turn them on to healthier foods.

The following lists offer some ideas for meals and snacks for your toddler (*recipes can be found at the end of this book!*). These meal ideas cover an age where your child is growing and changing rapidly. Younger toddlers will naturally eat smaller amounts than older toddlers and they will need their food cut up into pieces that are appropriately sized.

Remember: <u>Never</u> leave your toddler unattended while they are eating to prevent choking!

Breakfasts For Toddlers

1.) Unsweetened breakfast cereal topped with banana, raisins, and full fat milk
2.) Full fat yoghurt topped with berries and unsweetened granola
3.) Scrambled eggs, toast, and a glass of fruit juice
4.) Oatmeal made with full fat milk and sweetened with a teaspoon of good quality fruit jam

5.) French toast with cinnamon (no need for sugar or syrup!) with chopped apple or pear

Lunches For Toddlers

1.) Hummus with pita bread dippers, cucumbers and tomatoes
2.) Baked beans and toast with a small cup of orange juice
3.) Cream cheese and marmite sandwich with a piece of fruit
4.) Small shapes of pasta with homemade marinara sauce
5.) Bean dip with breadsticks, carrots, and celery

Dinners For Toddlers

1.) Steamed carrots and broccoli with cheesy mashed potatoes
2.) Homemade pizza bites with mushrooms
3.) Cheese and bean quesadillas with cucumbers and tomatoes on the side
4.) Baked beans with cornbread and sweet potato fries
5.) Spinach and butternut squash risotto topped with cheese

Snacks For Toddlers

1.) Celery topped with favourite nut butter and raisins
2.) Carrot sticks, cucumbers, and breadsticks with hummus
3.) Apple sticks dipped in peanut butter (or other nut butter)
4.) Dried fruit like apricots, figs, or dates
5.) Rice cakes topped with nut butter, marmite, tahini, hummus, or cream cheese
6.) Hard-boiled eggs
7.) Cut up melon, orange wedges, or grapes
8.) Cheese and crackers
9.) Toast with Marmite

10.) Yoghurt or fromage frais

At the end of the book you will find a number of recipes to help get you inspired but remember to have fun with food. Try out new recipes and new ingredients regularly and let your little one get involved. Diets that include a variety of different foods are healthier and more interesting for everyone in the household. Remember, it doesn't really matter how much your child eats in one sitting as long as they're getting everything they need throughout the day. Before I move on to the next age group, here's a few top tips for feeding your toddler.

15 Top Tips For Toddlers

1.) Feed your child the same food you are eating if and where possible. This is easier for you when it comes to cooking and your toddler will be more happy to try new things if they see you eating them!

2.) Think of milk as food and be careful not to give too much of it as this may make your child too full for solids.

3.) Make every food count! Steer clear of snacks and drinks that are not nutritionally beneficial as this may make your child too full for the healthy foods! Think of snack time as an extra opportunity for nutrients.

4.) Be careful not to offer your child too much fruit juice as its high sugar content can be bad for your child's teeth and blood sugar levels.

5.) Make fruit-based smoothies a *treat,* not an everyday food. When fruit is blended, its natural sugars are released and this means that smoothies can do the same damage to teeth as a full sugar soft drink!

Vegetable-based smoothies are a healthier option for teeth and blood sugar levels and will reinforce how tasty vegetables can be!

6.) Offer your child a small piece of cheese after fruit to help remove excess sugar from their teeth.

7.) Offer water with every meal rather than allowing your child to get used to sugary drinks.

8.) In addition to having plenty of water to hand, give your child melon on warm days to keep them hydrated.

9.) Allow your child to feed themselves whenever possible as this helps them feel independent and keeps them interested in their food.

10.) Remember that your child has their own taste buds and will not necessarily like everything you do and this is fine! So too, our tastes change the older we get. Encourage your child to try new things regularly but respect their feelings if and where possible. They are humans with their own minds and opinions, something which should be encouraged. If they don't like something (within reason!), don't force them to eat it. You can always introduce that food again at a later date when they often feel differently about it. The most vital thing is not to make it into a huge stressful drama for them.

11.) Avoid processed foods that are full of salt, sugar, and preservatives.

12.) Avoid nut butters or spreads that contain corn syrup or high fructose contents.

13.) Use fresh fruit and vegetables wherever possible. If fresh ingredients aren't available, choose frozen options rather than canned.

14.) Try not to add any type of sweetener in your child's foods. If you are baking, choose recipes made with maple syrup, honey, or coconut palm sugar and always keep quantities to a minimum.

15.) If your child is going to someone else's home or a day care centre, inform them about your child's diet and send food with them to avoid any confusion or upset.

School Age Children and Teenagers

As our children enter their school days, their lives become more complex. Their social skills are developing at a constant rate, they're being exposed to new things every day, and learning about how other kids live. Unfortunately, in most schools the majority of children are meat-eaters and this can mean that your child stands out as being different. They will probably face a number of other kids who don't really understand their diet and this can cause upset from time to time.

School years are also a time when your child will begin branching out into the world. They will have clubs, classes, rehearsals, sports matches, field trips, and birthday parties in abundance. This means even more forums where your child might stand out. It can get tiring and stressful for kids (and parents) to feel like they have to defend their meal choices. It is up to the parents of vegetarian children to do their best to shield them from having negative experiences where food is concerned.

The best thing you can do to cope with the critics of the world is to plan ahead. If your child is going to a birthday party, for instance, talk to the parents in charge of the party and see what they're planning on serving. If there isn't going to be anything suitable for your child at the party, see if you can arrange to bring something ahead of time. Offer to make a few vegetarian dishes and make enough for the other kids as well. This approach tends to be much more subtle than packing a lunch for your child and telling them not to eat any of the party foods. If your child is put in a situation where they're supposed to be having fun and they end up having to explain their packed lunch to all the other kids, they're likely to feel frustrated or upset and they may not want to go to parties anymore.

Another situation that you and your child may find difficult is school lunches. If your child doesn't like the food at school, if there's limited options, or if you just prefer to pack their lunch, try not to give them things that they have to explain to other kids. We want to shield our children from negative attention and/or difficulties with other kids. When you pack your child's lunch, don't pack it with foods that are strange and usual. In order to attract less attention, stick to recognisable foods like sandwiches, bagels, pancakes, fruit, and maybe a small treat. Leave the exotic foods for home time! The same rules apply to field trips and any other packed lunch affair.

Although planning ahead can really help reduce the amount of negative attention placed on your child's eating habits, it's also important to arm them with some clear and simple explanations for times they're placed in tricky situations. This way, if someone at school is challenging your child about their meal choices they can defuse the situation as quickly as possible. As there are many different reasons for being a vegetarian, it's wise to talk through *your* reasons with your child. Think about these things together and make a plan for facing adversity. For instance, my children and I are vegetarians because we're pacifists. We don't believe in killing animals for food and in this day and age, we believe that it's simply not necessary to do so. We have come up with a few short responses to common questions so that we don't have to embark on a conversational chess match every time someone challenges us. Have a look at the list below for some examples of how my children deal with unwanted challenges. Then think and talk with your child about some short responses that might work for them.

Facing Adversity & The Questions You Have To Answer

Challenge #1: But it's the food chain!

Answer: I believe in the food chain but I don't believe that humans are a part of it. Most animals act on instinct but humans have the ability to choose. I choose not to eat animals.

Challenge #2: But it's going to be killed anyway! You may as well just eat it!
Answer: Of course it is but I don't want to support the killing of animals by buying / eating them.

Challenge #3: But meat tastes so good. You don't know what you're missing!
Answer: You're right, I don't! Maybe that's why being a vegetarian is so easy for me!

Challenge #4: But animals were put on earth for us to eat them!
Answer: I don't believe that.

Challenge #5: You just want attention!
Answer: I just want to eat my lunch!

Remember to explain to your child that people can be judgmental about things they don't understand. Often meat-eaters take offence to vegetarianism because they think it's a comment on what *they* eat. This can lead to defensiveness and exhausting circular conversations. One of
my children's most effective responses is simply:

"Why are you so interested in what I eat? I don't care what *you* eat."

Works everytime!

How To Talk To Your Kids About Vegetarianism

Broaching the subject of vegetarianism with your children, whether they are new to it or it they have been vegetarian all their life, should be an easy thing to do but it can be difficult at times if not tackled correctly. Here are some guidelines you can follow.

1. Never Lie
Children are by nature naturally curious, so when they ask questions about what sausages are made from, or why you don't eat chicken, use the opportunity to tell the truth in a gentle way. Kids love animals and once they understand what being vegetarian really means they are able to easily comprehend the importance of it all.

2. Buy Vegetarian Friendly Kids Books
Thankfully there are a plenty of **vegetarian friendly books** around to help make your job a whole lot easier. Tackling tricky subjects with grace and clarity, books are a great vehicle to help you explore and explain vegetarian concepts in a compassionate and visually stimulating way.

3. Help Your Kids Feel Proud
Unfortunately there are still a lot of people that don't understand this type of lifestyle, so they make fun of it, and in turn can make your kids question their own beliefs and feel bad about their lifestyle. Encouraging your kids to feel proud of being vegetarian is a powerful tool in helping them to grow their confidence and affirm their choices.

4. Knowledge Is Everything!
Vegetarian education is key! It helps your kids understand the reasn behind vegetarianism, so make sure when you discuss the subject that you also teach them about the many benefits that come hand in hand with this lifestyle. From health to environmental, providing them with a well rounded view allows them to see the complete picture.

5. Visit A Local Farm Sanctuary
Taking a **trip to your local farm sanctuary** where you can spend time with all the beautiful animals and hear their stories will really help your family to make the connection. When your kids realize that farmed animals aren't happy, and in fact are often neglected and in pain, they won't be so quick to drink that glass of milk or tuck into

their egg sandwiches.

6. Point Out Vegetarian Role Models
Whether your kids are passionate about sports or they love music, these days there are thousands of vegertain athletes, musicians, movie stars and all sorts of other famous people for children to look up to and admire.

7. Have Fun In The Kitchen – Make the most of meal times and get your kids involved in the cooking and teach them about why you don't eat animal products along the way. Cooking should be a fun family experience and you can use it as an opportunity to get them excited about eating and experimenting with **delicious vegan food.**

Foods For School Age Children

Most kids go through a picky phase at some point in this stage of life. They love something one day and hate it the next. **This is natural!** These phases are common and they almost always resolve themselves in time. Unfortunately, having a picky eater in the house can cause unwanted stress and make mealtimes unbearable, if not dealt with correctly.

It's important to remember that children need quite a lot of nutrition and caloric intake but they don't have the same size stomachs as adults! Large meals could upset your child's stomach and make them reluctant at the dinner table, turning what should be a pleasant experience into one of stress and drama. The best way to be sure your child is getting everything they need without any extra drama is to allow them to eat many small meals throughout the day rather than three large meals. This doesn't mean that your child doesn't eat dinner with the family, it just means to lower your expectations at the dinner table. Give you child a smaller amount of food to start. Do away with the old fashioned belief that your child shouldn't eat between meals because they'll *"ruin their dinner"*. Think about what nutrition your child is taking in throughout the day rather than focusing your attention on one meal. Ensure that your child's small meals and snacks are nutritious and avoid sugary drinks (including fruit juice) wherever possible. Heavy liquids can fill your child's small stomach in no time!

If you're particularly focused on dinner, try to keep after school snacks on the smaller side. Remember the advice about toddlers regarding good experiences at mealtimes. Try not to nag your child! It will only upset everyone. Instead, do what you can to keep the mood light and your picky eater will probably grow out of their phase sooner rather than later. In addition, do what you can to ease your child's tension. For instance, if your child prefers raw carrots to cooked, let them have theirs raw! If you child doesn't like spicy food but you do, remove their portion before adding spice to the dish. Don't force them to eat something they don't want!

Forcing your child to eat things they genuinely don't like (or portions that are too large for them) could create a bad food relationship. Furthermore, if your child is being regularly encouraged to eat more than they're hungry for, they might develop a habit of ignoring their feelings of fullness and ending up overweight or unhealthy.

8 Top Tips For Picky Eaters

1.) Go grocery shopping together.
Shopping with your child gives you a great chance to check out new ingredients and talk about meals they might like to try. Be open to suggestions from your child.

2.) Cook together.
Encourage your child to join you in the kitchen and help you cook. This way they learn about kitchen safety, how to balance meals, and

how to cook while enjoying some bonding time with you. In addition, most children will always try something they've made themselves!

3.) Offer a few options.
Let your child choose between two or three meal options when possible so they feel like they have some control over the situation. Allowing your child to make choices is a great way of showing them respect. Children who are respected and who are encouraged to be part of decision making grow up to be confident, articulate, and wise.

4.) Resist a reward based system involving gifts, treats, or desserts.
Bribing your child to eat a meal only causes more stress in the future. It really is not worth it, do not fall into this tempting trap.

5.) Don't demonise or bully your child.
Punishing your child or making too big of a deal will only make meal times stressful for the whole family. When it comes to a picky eater, pick your battles rather than making a battle out of every single meal.

6.) Express yourself.
If your child eats more than usual or they finish a meal they wouldn't usually eat, praise them by telling them how that makes you feel. Try saying something like: "I'm so glad you ate all your dinner! I spent a long time making it and that's made me very happy."

7.) Look at the big picture.
Always judge what nutrients your child has consumed by looking at the whole day rather than one particular meal. A picky child will eventually grow out of it in their own time. The more relaxed you are about it, the quicker that will happen.

8.) Be realistic with your child's portion size.
Remember your child has a smaller stomach than you. Eating little and often is recommended for ultimate nutrition. Don't offer a

mountain of food at the start. Start small and offer more when that's finished.

Now that you've conquered picky eating and social situations, it's time for the good stuff. The following lists offer some ideas about meal planning for your school age child. Many of these recipes can be found at the end of this book.

Breakfasts for School Age Children

1.) Oatmeal with dried fruit and honey served with a glass of orange juice
2.) Banana pancakes with fresh blueberries and maple syrup served with a glass of milk
3.) Granola topped with yoghurt and strawberries
4.) Eggs "Any way", baked beans, and toast served with a glass of juice
5.) French Toast topped with bananas and a touch of honey with a glass of milk

Lunches for School Age Children

1.) Hummus and salad pita, a handful of pretzels, and an orange
2.) Grilled halloumi cheese and cucumber ciabatta with fruit salad, and chocolate milk
3.) Peanut butter and jelly sandwich, yogurt, and a banana
4.) Bagel with cream cheese, celery with peanut butter and raisins, and an apple
5.) Grilled cheese sandwich, tomato soup, and a granola bar

Dinners for School Age Children

1.) Mexican rice and beans topped with cheese, salsa, and avocado served with a green salad
2.) Cheese and spinach ravioli with steamed broccoli topped with homemade marinara sauce
3.) Veggie burgers, sweet potato fries, and corn on the cob
4.) Homemade pizza smothered with veggies served with a green salad
5.) Tofu "hotdogs" with macaroni and cheese, and peas

Snacks for School Age Children

1.) Veggie sticks with hummus
2.) A handful of nuts and seeds
3.) Frozen grapes
4.) Fresh fruit or berries
5.) A handful of homemade trail mix
6.) Toast with marmite and melted cheese
7.) Rice cakes with almond butter
8.) Breadsticks with white bean dip
9.) Banana-almond "milkshake"
10.) Fruit yoghurt

Exciting Foods for Teenagers

As I've mentioned in previous sections of this book, it is very important for your child's diet to include many different sources of vitamins and nutrients. This is particularly true with teenagers because of how rapidly they grow and change during this time of their lives. Making sure that your teenager's diet has plenty of variety is key to keeping them in top health. This is easier to accomplish if they have been raised vegetarian as they will have plenty of knowledge about vegetarian foods and well balanced meals; however, if your child is new to vegetarianism (as many teenagers are), you will need to pay close attention to their diet until they get the swing of things.

There are two common pitfalls that new vegetarians tend to fall into. They either over compensate for lost protein in their diet by eating too much cheese, peanut butter, or other fattening foods, or they simply don't replace the protein at all and live on things like potatoes, salad, and snacks. Remember that protein is not usually something to panic about and as long as your teenager's diet is varied, they're probably getting all they need. But, as I said earlier in this book, make sure to put plenty of focus on their other nutritional requirements. Vegetarian teenagers require plenty of *calcium, iron, and vitamin B12* so make sure your child's diet includes enough dairy, green vegetables, beans, legumes, and fortified cereals. Don't forget to serve iron-rich foods with vitamin C to ensure absorption.

The biggest battle that parents of teenagers face is keeping the intake of salty, sugary, or processed foods in check. Teenagers have a significantly increased appetite during the times their body is growing and changing at rapid rates. You have probably noticed your grocery bills have been getting larger and larger since the dawn of puberty! This next list offers some top tips to make sure your teenager gets the most out of their diet.

Top Tips for Teenagers

1.) Give foods that will provide long lasting energy.
Fruits, vegetable, and whole grains like brown rice, quinoa, oats, barley, and buckwheat provide long lasting energy and will help keep your teenager full for longer. This means that they're less likely to turn to unhealthy snacks between meals.

2.) Stress the importance of breakfast.
Breakfast is truly the most important meal of the day! Many teenagers rush out the door in the morning with an empty stomach. This could make them tired throughout the day, less alert in school, agitated, and prone to craving sugary, fattening foods. A teenager who starts the day with a hearty breakfast such as oatmeal or whole grain pancakes is more likely to have more energy through the day, higher test scores, and better moods.

3.) Plan ahead.
One of the easiest ways to prevent your teenager from turning to unhealthy snacks is to simply keep them supplied with healthy ones! Make a batch of protein bars or trail mix and encourage your teenager to carry them in their school bags.

4.) Always have healthy snacks available.
Fruit is an important facet to your teenager's diet but unfortunately it's not always their food of choice. Make sure that you always have fruit available at home and encourage your child to carry some with them when they're out. Combinations like apples and peanut butter or berries and yoghurt provide longer lasting energy than fruit on its own and may interest your teenager more! Other healthy snacks you can keep in your kitchen stocked with are hard boiled eggs, quinoa salads, hummus, and granola bars.

5.) Make the most of meals at home.
As your teenager gets older they will spend less and less time at home. They will pick up snacks and meals-to-go that you have little control over. Take every opportunity you can to provide your teen with well balanced, nourishing meals. Plan meals ahead of time and make it your mission to feed your teen well. Make green smoothies, healthier baked goods, and homemade snacks rather than stocking your cupboards with chocolate and fried snacks.

When in doubt, refer to to the following list of meal ideas!

Breakfasts for Teenagers

1.) Homemade breakfast bar, a banana, yoghurt, and orange juice
2.) Oatmeal with a cooked apple, and maple syrup
3.) Cheese and veggie omelette served with toast and fruit juice
4.) Breakfast burrito made with tofu scrambler, peppers, and tomatoes
5.) Buckwheat pancakes with berries and maple syrup with homemade breakfast juice

Lunches for Teenagers

1.) Triple-decker sandwich with hummus, avocado, tomatoes, and bean sprouts with pretzels and veggie juice
2.) Quinoa and butternut squash salad, a granola bar, veggie sticks, and fruit
3.) Cheese and salad roll, yoghurt, a piece of fruit, and a handful of nuts and seeds
4.) Baked beans, home fries, and toast with a glass of milk
5.) Homemade falafel, salad, and tahini dressing in a pita pocket

Dinners for Teenagers

1.) Black bean burritos with all the trimmings
2.) Vegetable curry with paneer, brown rice, and a green salad
3.) Veggie lasagne with garlic bread, and a butter bean salad
4.) Vegetable and tofu stir fry with brown rice
5.) Roasted mediterranean vegetable quiche, baked potato, and root vegetable "fries"

Snacks for Teenagers

1.) Green smoothie
2.) Yoghurt with granola
3.) Homemade protein bar
4.) Cheese and crackers
5.) Handful of nuts and seeds
6.) English muffin with melted cheese
7.) Chick pea crunchies
8.) Hummus, pita, and veggies
9.) Corn chips with salsa and guacamole
10.) Toast with almond butter

Part Three: The Recipes

Now that you're well equipped to raise a healthy, happy vegetarian, it's time to get cooking! Here are all the recipes I referred to earlier. Most of these can be altered to suit you and your child's tastes so feel free to get creative with them! Cooking is an absolute must for vegetarian parents. Not only does it ensure that you know what's in your child's food, but cooking at home also saves you money! One thing you will notice, is that I often encourage you to "sneak" extra goodness into your recipes. These little tricks are great for children who are going through picky phases!

Perfect Every Time Granola

Ingredients:
1 1/3 cups jumbo oats
1/3 cup cashews
1/4 cup pumpkin seeds
1/4 cup sunflower seeds
2 tbsp sesame seeds
2 tbsp chia seeds
3 tbsp coconut oil
1/4 cup maple syrup
1/4 cup honey
1 tsp vanilla
1/3 cup dried cranberries
1/4 cup desiccated coconut

Method:
Preheat oven to 300 degrees (F) / 150 degrees (C). Combine all wet ingredients together. Add the oats, nuts, and seeds and mix well. Spread the mix over one or two baking trays and bake for 15 minutes. Remove from the oven, add cranberries and coconut and return to the oven for a further 15 minutes. Cool and store in an airtight container.

Raw Power Breakfast Bars

Ingredients:
1 1/2 cup jumbo oats
1/2 cup cashews
1/4 cup walnuts
1/4 cup pumpkin seeds
1 cup pitted dates
1/4 cup maple syrup
1/4 cup almond butter
1 tsp cinnamon
1/2 tsp ground ginger
1/4 tsp nutmeg
1 tsp vanilla
1 tbsp molasses

Method:
Line a 9 inch square baking pan with plastic wrap. Breakdown the dates in a food processor until you have a dough like mixture. Combine with oats, nuts, and seeds. Heat the almond butter, spices, vanilla, and molasses in a sauce pan and add it to the mix thoroughly. Press the mix into the baking pan and refrigerate for 30 minutes. Cut into squares and store in the refrigerator for a week.

Buckwheat Pancakes

Ingredients:
1 cup buckwheat flour
2 tbsp brown sugar
1 tsp baking powder
1/2 tsp baking soda
1/2 tsp salt
1 egg

1 cup buttermilk
1 tbsp melted butter
1/2 teaspoon cinnamon (optional)
one half of a ripe banana (optional)*

Method:
Combine dry and wet ingredients separately, then mix together being careful to avoid over mixing. Ladle batter into a med/hot pan coated with cooking spray. Cook until small bubbles appear, then flip over. Serve with berries and maple syrup.
If making banana pancakes, reduce buttermilk to 1/4 cup.

Tofu Scrambler

Ingredients:
2 blocks extra-firm tofu
2 tablespoons olive oil
1 small onion, chopped
1 small green pepper, chopped
1 small red bell pepper, chopped
1/2 tsp ground coriander
1/2 tsp ground cumin
1 1/2 tsp ground turmeric
1 can black beans drained and rinsed
2 tbsp fresh coriander, chopped
sat and pepper to taste

Method:
Drain water from tofu and press between paper towels or muslin to remove excess moisture. Heat the oil in a pan at med/high heat. Add onions and peppers. Heat for 3 minutes, stirring occasionally. Add in spices, tofu, and beans and heat for a further 2 or 3 minutes. Add the fresh coriander and mix through. Remove from heat and serve with toast or wrapped in a tortilla.

Best Homemade Hummus

Ingredients:
1 can chick peas
1 clove garlic
2 tbsp tahini
juice of 1/2 a lemon
1/2 teaspoon ground cumin (optional)
1 tbsp tamari or soy sauce
3 tbsp olive oil
1/4 cup water (as needed)

Method:
Combine all ingredients (except water) in a food processor and blend for one minute. Add water gradually as needed to achieve desired consistency. Blend for 3 more minutes or until smooth. Sprinkle with paprika and a drizzle of olive oil to serve.

*Substitute any white beans for chick peas to make an alternative dip.

Quinoa and Butternut Squash Salad

Ingredients:
1 small butternut squash, peeled and cubed
4 tbsp olive oil
1 clove garlic, crushed
1 teaspoon herbs de provence
1 teaspoon smoked sea salt
1 cup quinoa, soaked for 1-3 hours and rinsed
2 cups vegetable stock or water
juice of 1/2 lemon
small handful of fresh herbs like marjoram, basil, or parsley

Method:

Preheat oven to 375 degrees (F) / 190 degrees (C). Combine butternut squash, 2 tablespoons of olive oil, garlic, herbs de provence and sea salt and bake on a baking tray bake for 20-30 minutes until squash is soft but not mushy. Bring the quinoa and stock to boil in a pot, stirring occasionally. Simmer until the stock is absorbed and remove from heat. Finally, mix together the squash and quinoa. Drizzle with the remaining 2 tbsp olive oil and lemon juice. Sprinkle with fresh herbs and serve.

Mexican Rice and Beans

Ingredients:
1 cup brown rice (soaked for 1-3 hours and rinsed)
1 small onion, chopped
2 or 3 cloves garlic, chopped
1 red pepper, chopped (optional)
1 can black beans, drained and rinsed
2 1/2 cups vegetable stock
2 tbsp tomato puree
1 1/2 tsp cumin
1 tsp ground coriander
1/2 tsp chilli powder (optional)
salt and pepper to taste
small handful of fresh coriander, chopped

Method:
Heat oil in a pan on med/high heat. Add onions and sweat for a minute, then add peppers and garlic and heat for another minute. Add rice and stir. Heat for another minute. Add the remaining ingredients except black beans and fresh coriander. Bring to a boil. Reduce to a simmer and cook, covered for 15 minutes stirring occasionally. Add beans and cook for a further 10 minutes. Add water to rice if needed. When rice is well cooked and cooking liquid is gone, remove from heat stir in fresh coriander. Serve with a salad, in a burrito, or as a filling for tacos.

Marinara Sauce

Ingredients:
2 tablespoons olive oil
4 cans of chopped tomatoes
1 can full of vegetable stock (measure in one of the empty tomato cans!)
4 cloves of garlic, minced
1 onion, finely chopped
6 "cubes" frozen spinach or a few handfuls of chopped, fresh spinach (optional)
1/2 cup of dry red lentils (optional)
1 whole celery stalk
1 whole carrot
3 teaspoons dried basil or 4 teaspoons chopped, fresh basil (or to taste)
1 1/2 teaspoons of dried oregano or 2 teaspoons chopped, fresh oregano (or to taste)
salt and pepper to taste

Method:
Heat the olive oil over medium/high heat in a large pot and add the onions. Allow them to sweat for a minute and then add the garlic and heat for 30 seconds. Then add the lentils and stir to coat them in the flavoured oil for 30 seconds to a minute. Next add the tomatoes, stock, and herbs. Place the carrot and celery stalk in whole. This is a great way to take some of the bitterness out of the tinned tomatoes! Bring the sauce to a simmer and allow to cook, uncovered, for 20 - 30 minutes, stirring regularly. When your sauce has reduced by about 1/3, remove it from the heat, remove the carrot and celery, and puree the sauce with a hand blender. You will notice that if you are using lentils, your sauce will be thick and "creamy". Serve this sauce with spaghetti, lasagne, or as an extra healthy pizza sauce!

Pesto (with added nutrients!)

Ingredients:
2 handfuls of fresh basil
1 handful baby spinach or chard
1/4 cup of olive oil
2 tablespoons of toasted pine nuts or walnuts ("toast" by heating in a dry pan)
1 centimetre cube of parmesan cheese
1/2 clove of garlic
salt and pepper to taste

Method:
Blitz all ingredients in a food processor. Taste and add salt if necessary. Increase the olive oil to your individual taste too! Use this on pasta, bruschetta, as a pizza sauce, or as a flavour enhancer for any other Italian cooking or hummus. Alternatively, increase the amount of olive oil and store in a tall, lidded jar to use as a dip for breads and crackers.

Banana-Almond "Milkshake"

Ingredients:
1 1/2 ripe bananas
1 1/2 cups cold almond milk
1 tbsp honey
small handful of blueberries (optional)

Method:
Combine all ingredients in a blender and blend until smooth. Garnish with a strawberry or sprig of mint.

Green (but tasty) Smoothie

Ingredients:
1 handful of fresh kale or spinach
1 1/2 ripe bananas
1/2 cup blueberries
1 1/2 cup apple juice
agave nectar to taste (optional)

Method:
Combine all ingredients except agave nectar in blender and blend very well. Add agave nectar as you like. Garnish with sliced strawberries and serve ice cold.

Raising Happy, Healthy Vegetarian Children

Raising a happy, healthy vegetarian child isn't rocket science and it doesn't have to be difficult. Vegetarian children are not "missing out" on anything but sometimes the world around them can be challenging. Take your child's health seriously. Plan their meals and keep an eye on snacks! Have fun together in the kitchen. Maintain an open dialogue with your child about why you eat the way you do. This will help prepare your child when they are faced with the opinions of others. Encourage your child to cook and shop with you and try not to be disappointed if they go through a picky phase!

Remember, vegetarian children are healthy children. Their diets are varied and delicious. They have been found to be of a higher IQ than meat-eating children, and have been proven to have significantly reduced risks of diabetes, obesity, high blood pressure, heart disease, and certain cancers!

Your vegetarian child is getting a fantastic start to life. Be proud!

CPSIA information can be obtained at www.ICGtesting.com
Printed in the USA
BVOW05s0216210616

452843BV00023B/143/P